Building Business One Cup of Coffee at a Time

Jan Verhoeff

Let's do Coffee!

Copyright @ Jan Verhoeff, 2019

All rights reserved. No portion of this book may be reproduced in any form or by any electronic or mechanical means, including information storage and retrieval systems, without express permission from the author, except by a reviewer who may quote brief passages in a review.

Published in the United States of America by JV Publications.

www.JVPublications.com

Verhoeff, Jan

Building Business One Cup of Coffee at a Time...

1st edition, February, 2019

ISBN: 9781795619028

PRINTED IN THE UNITED STATES OF AMERICA

10 9 8 7 6 5 4 3 2 1

Cover design, book design/layout by JV Publications

Thank you for buying this

ACE Writers book.

To receive special offers, bonus content, and info on new releases and other great reads, sign up for our newsletters.

Or visit us online at acewriters.com/newsletters

For email updates on the author, click JanVerhoeff.com

The author and publisher have provided this book for your personal use only. You may not make this book publicly available in any way. Copyright infringement is against the law. If you believe this copy infringes on the author's copyright, please notify the publisher at: acewriters.com/piracy

Contents

Let's do Coffee! 3
Acknowledgements 11
Introduction 13
Billionaires Are Created Out of Brainstorming Sessions 15
    Brainstorming in a group is a great way to inspire ideas. 15
    What seeds come out of your conversations? 17
Blessings Come Whether We Deserve Them or Not 21
Business Today - 31
    Innovation is the heart of capitalism. 31
    We are taught the power of business ownership in Proverbs 31. 32
    Business today is an open door to change the world. 33
    She wisely extolled him to be worthy of such a woman. 34
    So, here's the outtake on this whole Business Today Concept. 36

Capitalism allows us to independently choose wealth.........37

Business today is an open opportunity to build greater independence. 37

Online Entrepreneurs Open the Door to Capitalism........39

Small Businesses Change Lives........39

What's your value as an entrepreneur?........41

What's Coffee Got to Do with Building a Business?........43

   It didn't happen often. 43

   The result was the same........43

   Building Websites........44

   But can you use the coffee concept? 45

   Encourage and Motivate 46

About the Author 49

Acknowledgements

This is where I'm supposed to dedicate this book and these articles to those spectacular folks who have unselfishly supported my efforts as an author over the past few months while I worked determinedly to complete this incredible piece of literary genius. The truth, nobody really wanted me to do this. Nobody will probably read it. And to be more specific, none of you will likely offer a review of this work, because you're too busy pretending to be someone you aren't, holding out that you already know what's in here, or worse… pretending to be supportive. The publisher believes it's just another book on the bookstore shelf. The readers like the cover so much that they're going to buy it to show off on their coffee table, but they'll probably never flip a page.

And then…

I'm short a significant other who probably would just be upset that I spent so much time putting this together when he wasn't interested in it anyway.

My kids will read it, after I'm gone, but I doubt they'll pick up one before then, because they believe I've already taught them everything I know (boy are they gonna be surprised).

And my friends…

Some may read a page or two, but they'll claim they were too busy to read every single page I wrote, even though they'd have to ask me fewer questions about what I do if they'd open the book and read.

And my clients...

They pay for my words of wisdom and never listen. They sign up for my content and never read it. They'll probably buy this and put it on a shelf with the rest of my books and wonder why they aren't making any money online.

I'd tell them, if they'd only read the book.

So, I'm acknowledging the barking dogs next door that kept me up late enough at night to write this many words, and the chill in the air that encouraged me to keep moving, and the words and ideas that inspired me to put them on paper. Maybe someday... These words will be valuable to someone.

God bless you, my reader.

Introduction

Kevin Cullis opened a door recently, and invited me to write an article for his next book coming out shortly. I've written a couple of valuable articles, and submitted them. Business Today is a culmination of several of those articles, but more... It's the whole of the purpose for which I'm writing. However, in the process that is our day to day discussion of articles, he or I missed the part that those articles were for his book...

And I ended up publishing them elsewhere.

The result of that published elsewhere little thingie is that I realize I'd created a good sized collection of articles that should have been published in one unit, but they were scattered to the winds of the Internet. Most of them not really generating the results that would have benefited and blessed people the most, because they were so scattered.

In that vein, I decided this next attempt will be a bit different than previous submissions, because he doesn't care if it's published or not...

Business Today was published on my personal blog, and I've gathered the other articles to publish them all in this collection, where you can get the most of this concept called Walking in Faith.

And I have good reason to publish on this topic here in the book. So... I'm writing the expose here, sharing all the articles, and giving Kevin the full-introspective article for *his* book, the relevance of the Business Today article as he requested.

Enjoy the glimpse of Business Today and how it affects business startups, entrepreneurs, and online entrepreneurs the world over.

We're in the center of the climb here...

We can either keep going, building strong capitalism features around the world, and push back against the ills of socialistic, communism, or cave to the demands of the malicious one world order.

Or we can free fall to the death of the world.

The choice is ours, one entrepreneur at a time.

We climb.

Or we fall.

But here's how it's done!

Billionaires Are Created Out of Brainstorming Sessions

Bezos wasn't a Billionaire when he got the idea for Amazon.com. And Elon probably had a host of engineers sitting around the table when Tesla was born. Ideas for business inspire new billionaires every single day.

Will your next idea be the birth of a billionaire?

> *"Truthful living will make you think in new directions, learn with greater desire, and achieve your highest potential." ~Jeffrey Gitomer*

Brainstorming in a group is a great way to inspire ideas.

Writers groups come together to read each other's books, write reviews, and edit the end results of writing endeavors. Their results are often published.

Business owners and entrepreneurs often come together to brainstorm new business ideas, or talk about ideas needed to sustain their own businesses.

When the "local shops were closing" due to Walmart's inept servitude, a comment generated out of frustration – "If only there were a mail order Walmart... That would be Amazing!" And Amazon was born. Was Amazon.com a direct response to that comment? Maybe, maybe not.

Did it inspire Amazon.com? In a very real way, and for very personal reasons, I'm going to say that comment was a seed.

What seeds come out of your conversations?

It's been said, "There's nothing new under the sun." And I'm a firm believer in that concept. Anything we do, has been done before in one way or another. So, thinking up some new concept, or worrying out a new idea, probably isn't really NEW to anyone, but rather just a recalculated method of reaching the end goal.

Entrepreneurs are born every day, many of them are born at the round table when an inspiration turns on the light.

At a brainstorming session a few weeks ago, a business owner said, "I wish I had a thought manager to sort out all these ideas we've come up with today. If we just had a way to sort them out, organize them into businesses, and channel them to the right people… All kinds of new businesses could be born."

Poof! It happened. A Thought Manager was formulated, born, and created. From nothing but a slew of words spewed forth at the round table… The discussion that ignited the thought manager continues almost every week, and the conversation is noted and will ultimately be published as blog posts, after curating it for feasible ideas. But isn't that what business is all about?

Bezos came up with an amazing mail order version of the Big Box Store. Elon created a stellar electric auto. And business in the real world vibrates with energy.

Are business ideas really greater than talents? What are you doing with the talents God has given you?

> *Matthew 25:15 To one he gave five talents, to another two talents, and to another one talent— each according to his own ability. And he promptly went on his journey.*

Are you listening? Do you have ideas coming at you at the speed of light on a daily basis? Have you heard them? Do you ever implement them?

What would happen, if you implemented just one idea a month, for a new business? Then sold that idea... Would you benefit? Would life become better because more small businesses are being created, increasing jobs, gross national product, and services in our communities? How much could you improve your life if you simply acted on or shared one idea per month?

If your ideas are billionaire makers... Who will benefit?

Blessings Come Whether We Deserve Them or Not

Many years ago, I posted the Prayer of Jabez on the wall over my desk. A tiny scrap of paper, with the words copied in my own hand at first, then a sticky note, and later a printed page with the words in black font on white paper. More recently, I've gotten creative and posted the words in a colorful graphic design with a nice black frame around them.

But the message, a powerful prayer from Chronicles in the Bible, has been my heart's desire for more years than I remember.

Oh that thou wouldest bless me indeed, and enlarge my coast, and that thine hand might be with me, and that thou wouldest keep me from evil, that it may not grieve me!

The story, as told in I Chronicles 4:9 is that Jabez was more honorable than his bothers, and his mother named him Jabez, saying "Because I bare him with sorrow." So when he was grown, he uttered these famous words of prayer, that God would bless him, INDEED. And enlarge his coast, and be with him, to keep him from evil that he might not be grieved.

Jabez didn't want to feel the sorrow his mother felt in baring him. He wanted God's blessing. Jabez sought hard after God's blessing, and although he didn't believe he earned it, he believed he would receive it.

Do you believe?

Do you look about at what others have suffered and ask for God's blessing over you, that you might not suffer as they have?

I remember in the early days of my prayer, I struggled mightily with being a single mom (my husband left when my children were young), owning my business, and raising my children. It was my greatest desire that my children not suffer the horrific fates I'd seen in other children raised by single moms. I prayed fervently that God would intercede on their lives, and bring my children closer to Him each and every day. And I prayed the prayer of Jabez, "Oh Lord, bless me indeed, and enlarge my coast!"

At the time, we lived in a small town, and I longed for views of the Rocky Mountains. I longed to live where I could see mountain views, sunrise, sunsets, and beautiful skies. Our first home outside that small town was a condo overlooking the west side of Denver metro area, with views of the Rocky Mountains in the distance. The Front Range, west of the city, offered VAST open views, and I felt blessed beyond my wildest dreams.

I believed God would answer my prayers. And he did.

I learned. I realized, I had to believe when I asked God to provide. And more than anything else, I began to understand that I could ask of him ANYTHING. Absolutely nothing was outside the realm of being, if I asked for it. God would provide whatever I asked. I just had to open up my view and ASK for what I needed, and BELIEVE He would provide it.

Are you faithful?

If you have faith, as a mustard seed....

That's really not very much faith. When you think about it, faith in the amount of a mustard seed, almost anyone can do that much faith. But what about bigger. What about if I have faith the size of a watermelon? Will it be more? Will the results be bigger?

And what if I choose not only to have faith, but also to remain faithful... No matter what? If I'm faithful to believe, to do what I must, and continue to be faithful to keep God's word, and keep being grateful, no matter what? What if I choose to faithfully, believe, and hold onto God's promise, even when things look bleak or dark? What if, I choose to remain FAITHFUL?

Are you faithful?

I chose to be faithful, even when the days were darkest... And trust me, there were some really DARK days during that time period. Yet, still, I remained faithful, dedicated to seeking God's face even in the darkest hours.

I chose to remain faithful. I chose to have greater faith, even when all seemed to be loss, I remained faithful to the promise that God would provide.

And He did.

Sometimes in the final hour, but God always provided.

I did the work, and God provided the solutions, the answers, and the means of survival that we needed.

But then, I realized...

God wants more for me than to "survive".

Ask and You WILL Receive.

I'd managed to work my way into a tither. In all the struggles of achieving my dreams, I'd been "going it alone" determined to achieve, and although I continued the Prayer of Jabez, and studied my Bible faithfully, I realized I was missing something. I was missing something important.

Business was good. My children were raised. And I'd stepped out in faith into a job I really hadn't been excited about, but... It appeared to be right.

Slowly the revelation that I had stepped off the path, and I wasn't where I needed to be spiritually. I had no fellowship, and I was beginning to complain, instead of feeling gratitude. When I realized I'd lost my ability to feel gratitude, there was more... I'd forgotten that tiny little thing about being FAITHFUL to be GRATEFUL in ALL things.

I'd forgotten to be faithful.

There was more than a mustard seed of faith inside that God was still providing, but the big issue was that I wasn't being faithful to my part of this huge deal. I wasn't feeling, or expressing my gratitude in anything. I'd abandoned my responsibility to do what I was called to do, which was to be faithful.

STILL, God's provision stood firm. He continued to provide for my needs.

And I hadn't really asked.

Oh, I'd prayed the words... But I hadn't ASKED God to provide what I needed, or even been grateful for what was provided.

Then, someone reminded me that God's provision isn't based on my actions, but rather on His promise.

Proverbs 10:22 "The blessing of the Lord – it makes rich, and He adds no sorrow with it."

There is no COST to the riches God provides us. His provision comes without cost. We don't have to toil or EARN what God provides.

The Bible says ASK and you will Receive.

Matthew 7:7 King James Version (KJV) *Ask and it will be given to you; seek and you will find; knock and the door will be opened to you.*

God's promises are true. His assurances are many. And His word is unbroken. My friends, you may feel like I'm preaching a sermon here, but it's more... I'm sharing God's Holy word with you, and the whole value that is provided within the constraints of what has happened with my own life, and how God's provision really works. And it really DOES work. God provides very well when we allow him to do so, and look to him for guidance as to how we might better use the amazing skills and talents He's provided us.

Yes, I firmly believe that some of His provision comes by way of talents and ways to use the many talents he's given us.

But yet, still... There's that toil thing...

God promises He will add no sorrow with His blessing. Which means He won't make us toil to earn the blessing. But the work we get to do while earning our way in this world won't be difficult or cause sorrow, if its work ordained by the designer of our skills and talents. God will make it pleasurable.

And that my good friends is the message I want you to hear through this commentary, loud and clear.

God will bless you in ways that fulfill the desires of your heart, when your heart desires Him. And He'll do it in such a way that you find pleasure in putting forth the effort to earn those blessings. And better yet, my friends, He'll bless you abundantly without you even asking Him... But make it a point to ask for what you want, and seek out His desires for your life. The benefits will amaze you!

Proverbs 10:22 Amplified Bible, Classic Edition (AMPC) *The blessing of the Lord—it makes [truly] rich, and He adds no sorrow with it [neither does toiling increase it].*

Let's talk about those talents and skills, and what you can do with them to benefit you even more.

Business Today -

My soul follows hard after Thee
Early in the morning will I rise up and seek Thee
And because Thou hast been my help
Under the shadow of Thy wing
I will rejoice.

This morning, I was out of cream for my coffee, so I added a small pat of butter. I really can't stand black coffee. It's just too sharp for my taste, and although the butter isn't cream, it softens the sharpness of the coffee and I relish the texture on my tongue.

Innovation is the heart of capitalism.

Without innovation, as a population, we stagnate, falter, and die off, for lack of sustenance. Doing the same old thing for eons may provide the basic needs of our peoples, but ultimately if we remain in the same tiny pool of existence, the gene pool is decimated and death is the result. Businesses that refuse to grow, die. People who refuse to learn and change, die. The basis, the foundation, the fundamental reality of business today is growth. We must grow. As a business, as people, as entrepreneurs, we must grow.

We are created for growth, change, evolution, and survival. The fittest among us grow best, because they adapt to required changes.

We are taught the power of business ownership in Proverbs 31.

In Proverbs 31:3, King Lemuel is taught by his mother who raised him up to be a King, *³ Give not thy strength unto women, nor thy ways to that which destroyeth kings.* She was a wise woman who taught him such great wisdom. In verse 10, she teaches him that to find a wise woman, a woman who is born of equal value, he must choose carefully, ¹⁰ᵇ *for her price is far above rubies.*

She goes on to teach Lemuel what a good woman is, and how she will lead her nation. This isn't a woman alone, or a woman without the sustenance of a husband, or God. His mother teaches him that his woman, the wise woman he will choose is a hard worker who will prepare for the winter. She teaches Lemuel that she will respect him, will honor him, and that HE will be great.

His mother lifts him up into the arms and heart of a great woman, by acknowledging his greatness in the city where: *[23] Her husband is known in the gates, when he sitteth among the elders of the land.* And in the end of the book of Proverbs 31, we are taught the whole value of being a business owner, just as his mother taught Lemuel, *[31] Give her of the fruit of her hands; and let her own works praise her in the gates.*

When you build your business, the fruits of your efforts will bring praise to you. You are blessed by the work you do, the benefit you provide to others, and the great efforts you make to serve in your business [nation].

Business today is an open door to change the world.

Are you an innovator? Do you innovate ideas? Do you seek answers by finding problems and solving those problems? And do you allow the words of

Proverbs 31 to lead and guide you as a son of the most high? For so many years, I equated the Proverbs 31 woman with who I should be as a woman, and I dove right into that process, being the best mother I could be, serving my family, my community, my business, as I was told to do in the Book of Proverbs. And I continue to reap the great benefits of having been a Proverbs 31 woman.

But there's so much more to that book than directives to women. The directives were not to women in that book of the Bible. Those directives were from a woman, Lemuel's mother, to Lemuel, the King. She told him to find such a woman. And more...

She wisely extolled him to be worthy of such a woman.
As a woman, do you meet the requirements laid out by Lemuel's mother to qualify to be his wife?

As a man, have you made yourself worthy of such a woman?

While Proverbs 31 is most decidedly about the whole value of a man finding a woman who reflects his wealth in the city, the more important aspect of this Book of the Bible, as it relates to Business Today, is the wealth of information it provides for a business owner. And most of that wealth is literally found in the last line of the chapter.

> *Give her of the fruit of her hands;*
> *and let her own works praise her in the gates.*

This my friends, is the epitome of Capitalism. There is no option here for socialism, or for sharing the wealth of others, or with others. The command is to give her the fruits of her hands, and let her own works praise her in the gates. Are you listening? Do you hear this?

While earlier in the chapter, she is commanded to provide for others. Proverbs 31:20 says, "*She stretcheth out her hand to the poor; yea, she reacheth forth her hands to the needy.*" So, she does provide for those in need, by virtue of what SHE offers them. Yet, she offers to them. She gives as she sees fit, and it is not taken from her to give to the poor and needy.

So, here's the outtake on this whole Business Today Concept.
Business Today for Online Entrepreneurs Offers a Foundation of Innovative Solutions

Our deep joy is found in the power of providing solutions, of giving ourselves into our business as whole, complete, and empowered individuals capable of serving others on the basis of our ability to be independent. When we lose the power to independently make decisions, choose the direction we take, and build businesses out of our own choices, we've lost more than our political freedom. We've given up the power to live.

Capitalism allows us to independently choose wealth.

Wealth isn't necessarily a dollar figure. Money is a good thing, and without it, you won't have the ability to accomplish the good things you'd like to accomplish. But you'll learn rather quickly in a world without capitalism that wealth is something FAR different than dollar value. Wealth is a state of mind. Wealth is the ability to be independent, innovative, and inspired. And more than anything else wealth is a result of capitalism, not socialism.

There is no redistribution of "wealth" that equates to sharing your innovative self. You can't SHARE your independence. You can't SHARE inspiration. But, you CAN inspire others to be innovative, independent, and build on those individual choices.

Business today is an open opportunity to build greater independence.

A key function of the internet is the process of opening doors and showing a whole world of individuals that anyone who has a good idea can make that idea greater. Individuals can invite other individuals to share the process of growing businesses, innovating solutions, and building on the ideas of liberty. When we're free to think independently, share those thoughts, and grow greater, better, more amazing businesses as a result of sharing ideas through mentoring groups, round table discussions, and mastermind dumps, the outcomes are bigger and better. We grow in these open spaces where we're free to be individuals, sharing thoughts with other individuals.

Imagine the concept of a dozen people in a room innovating ideas for businesses, and then each of them taking from that round table discussion the idea that resonates with them to the forefront of the marketing place.

Incredible, unbelievably successful businesses are born of these!

Online Entrepreneurs Open the Door to Capitalism

When people talk about global markets, a global economy, or even global wealth, they aren't always talking about one world order. In this case, we're talking about individuals who have opened the door to dynamic interactive discussions of what needs can be filled with businesses developed around the world, and solutions innovated by individuals to fulfill those needs. Nationalism, the ability of each nation to be successful in and of itself is imperative for these individual business entities to survive.

The creation of pockets of industry, small businesses of enterprising and innovative idea launchers, and cottage industries where products are built and sold, bring local wealth and sustenance. Communities of individuals building businesses that inspire success support the economy.

Small Businesses Change Lives

Where is your small business located?

Are you in Brazil, where coffee grows well, providing quality coffee for a small coffee shop in North America? Or maybe Greenland? They can't grow coffee in Greenland, but they brew a fine blend of coffee in a coffee shop where drillers,

and snow bound philosophers gather to inspire the people of Australia to find a solution for the spider population and overgrowth of webs. Or perhaps, you're a wheat farmer in the USA feeding the people of Africa who are suffering through a drought? Maybe, you live in the deserts of Africa and have woven fine cloth from a grass that grows only in the driest of deserts, but that cloth is warm and thick, providing needed buffering for a Siberian winter?

What small business can you build that will CHANGE LIVES around the world?

This is not a global economy.

It is a local business that sells on a global market.

Be inspired to use what you have to build your local economy, your personal wealth, and worldwide solutions!

What's your value as an entrepreneur?

As a blogger, my goal is to inspire the world, one person at a time. Every single person who reads my blog walks away with something... Inspired? I hope. An innovative idea that will change lives? I pray. A renewed sense of independence, understanding that each and every person on this planet matters? That my friend, is my ultimate goal.

I want every single person who reads what I write to know she or he matters to me. I pray you're the one that solves the problems of the world. Do I dare hope that I inspired you to think that is possible?

You, my dearest friend, make a difference to me. You matter. I can only pray that you realize how much you matter, and how big an impact you can make, by being whom you are intended to be.

Your value as an entrepreneur is right there, inside of you, working to make a difference in your world.

Make that leap. The net will appear, and my friend. YOU make a difference.

What's Coffee Got to Do with Building a Business?

In the early days of building my online business, I was working from home with four kids playing in and around my office. Much of the time, I had one on my knee. So the opportunity to meet with a client at the local coffee shop was a welcome opportunity to escape home for fifteen minutes.

It didn't happen often.

I home schooled those four kids, and most of the time, I was a single parent. So leaving them home alone wasn't an option. By the time I'd found a coffee shop where I could take them with me, they were old enough to spend the time there studying, or reading, so we spent more time at the coffee shop, or at Barnes and Noble, or some other place where I could meet clients while they entertained themselves with reading or quiet work.

The result was the same.

I gained the benefit of escaping the walls of home, and my clients got the benefit of me – giving them a full range of business consulting in the time span of a cup or two of coffee (and one raspberry scone).

Then, eventually, as my clients became more and more long distance, a cup of coffee was an easy way for me to make $10 - $25 just answering a question.

More often than not, the one question was all it took to send a client off into his own version of success, and me back to work on my business.

But I knew if I answered a few "coffee questions" eventually, I'd have a full time consulting client paying for way more than my coffee. I offered plenty of value on those coffee talks, and invited them to take advantage of discounted consulting rates while on the call. Usually, they bought the plan, and we'd move on to the next phase of their business.

Building Websites

At first my web development business was a really cool secondary income. Then it moved into mainstream, and I enjoyed the blessings that came with writing web copy for startup businesses. Everyone wanted more professional looking pages, and I provided those at reasonable prices.

I had a way with words, and even the simplest word changes had a massive effect on the profitability of a small business with a new website. The key was using words that would effectively draw in business, and enable the business owner to sell their work without sounding, or being salesy.

I loved working with clients and most of my clients loved working with me. We had built relationships that would last, and clients often stuck it out with my web design company for ten or more years.

But can you use the coffee concept?

Anyone CAN use the coffee concept. And it's an excellent concept to use for starting up your online business. It creates a concept where you get paid for the initial consultation, not much, but something. And it's an opportunity for you to introduce the client to your paying programs.

If you're going to offer coaching or consulting, it's often easiest if you use something like the coffee concept to bring clients into your LIST.

That's an important part of the business building process. Build your list. Bring every customer into your list, and add them to your autoresponder, so they receive your email messages.

Email marketing is an easy way to increase the fundamental income of your business, and grow your tribe to a hungry group of participants who buy much of what you sell.

This is always a good idea. Because what you sell is going to be helpful to your buyers, and your buyers are going to inspire much of your program.

Encourage and Motivate

Maybe the biggest benefit I received or gave from the coffee concept was the encourage and motivate option. No matter how many times I had coffee with a client, I figured every time was an opportunity to encourage and motivate that client to accomplish their goals.

The secret that I used most was to simply ask what their goals were and write those down on the outside of my customer file. Then whenever I had an opportunity to do so, I'd ask how they were doing.

This did several things, but first and foremost, it let them know I'd heard them when they answered my question. Then it told them someone was pulling for them. And it reminded them to stay focused and working toward their goals.

Isn't it about time for coffee?

Let's do coffee soon and see where you need my help.

About the Author

Jan Verhoeff is a business consultant, business developer, and author. She lives and works in the greater Front Range area of Colorado. Her clients come from around the world.

She's the author of several books, among them:

Unstoppable: Caffeinated & Inspired

Be the Influencer in Your Niche

And others...

www.ingramcontent.com/pod-product-compliance
Lightning Source LLC
Chambersburg PA
CBHW031502210526
45463CB00003B/1032